The 60-Minute Active Training Series

How to Speak Up Without Putting Others Down

Participant's Workbook

Mel Silberman and Freda Hansburg

Published by Pfeiffer
An Imprint of Wiley
989 Market Street, San Francisco, CA 94103-1741   www.pfeiffer.com

For additional copies/bulk purchases of this book in the U.S. please contact 800-274-4434.

Pfeiffer books and products are available through most bookstores. To contact Pfeiffer directly call our Customer Care Department within the U.S. at 800-274-4434, outside the U.S. at 317-572-3985 or fax 317-572-4002 or www.pfeiffer.com.

Pfeiffer also publishes its books in a variety of electronic formats. Some content that appears in print may not be available in electronic books.

ISBN: 0-7879-7359-9

Acquiring Editor: Martin Delahoussaye

Director of Development: Kathleen Dolan Davies

Developmental Editor: Susan Rachmeler

Editor: Rebecca Taff

Senior Production Editor: Dawn Kilgore

Manufacturing Supervisor: Becky Carreno

Interior Design: Erin Zeltner

CONTENTS

ABOUT THIS BRIEF TRAINING SESSION

In the work world, there are many moments when people should speak up but are afraid to do so and, instead, suffer in silence. Sometimes, people are not afraid to speak up, but when they do, they show little tact and cause others to be defensive. This training session will help both people who are reluctant to speak up and those who do so with little tact.

At work, we need to express our opinions and our needs. Our opinions provide valuable input, feedback, and advice, but if held back, no one will benefit. And if expressed in a manner that makes others defensive, no one will listen to their value.

In order to be effective, at work and elsewhere, we must also have limits and establish those limits. If a person tries to be all things to all people, he or she will wind up disappointing others. We also need to be straightforward with our needs. Hinting at what we need from others only leads to disappointment and frustration. Once that happens, we often become angry with others and lose the calm and confidence we need to be at our best. People who are successful at asserting their needs are able to remain calm and confident, even when others try to provoke them and push their emotional buttons. They know how to stay focused on what it is they want to accomplish, how to express their needs directly, and how to respond effectively when others put on the heat.

You will have to opportunity:

- To discuss the benefits of speaking up

- To assess your assertion skills

- To identify work situations in which speaking up is essential

- To practice assertiveness in difficult situations

- To select "experiments in change" at work

How would you rate your ability to speak up without putting others down?

4 = consistently   3 = often   2 = sometimes   1 = never

___ 1. I let people know how I feel about important matters.

___ 2. I speak up when other people act in ways that limit my effectiveness.

___ 3. I can say no with grace and tact.

___ 4. I express my own views, even when I'm in the minority.

___ 5. I keep calm and remain confident when I get opposition.

THINKING ABOUT ASSERTIVENESS

1. When is it difficult to speak freely about your opinions and needs?

2. Why is it important to assert your opinions and needs?

3. How can you avoid putting others down or making them upset with you when you "speak up"?

When you assert your feelings and needs:

- Take a deep breath, slow yourself down, and talk just enough to express your wishes.

- Communicate your position, using phrases such as:

  "I would appreciate it if. . . .

  "I will not. . . ."

  "It would be great if. . . ."

  "I will have to. . . ."

  "Please. . . ."

  "I would prefer that. . . ."

  "It works best for me if. . . ."

  "I've decided not to. . . ."

- Give brief, nonapologetic explanations for your position. Stop talking after giving your reason.

  "I can't discuss it right now because I have a deadline to meet."

- Don't become defensive, or caught up in power struggles, or blow your cool.

- Repeat yourself like a "broken record," when necessary.

  Calmly restate what you've said.

  Say the same thing in new words.

- When you hear objections, use phrases like:

  "That may be."

  "We see it differently."

  "That's true, and. . . ."

  "I realize how important this is to you, and. . . ."

One situation in which I'd like to be more assertive about saying "no" or expecting someone else to do something I need is. . .

_____

_____

_____

_____

What exactly do I want in this situation? How insistent am I? What reasons would I give for my refusal or request?

_____

_____

_____

_____

_____

_____

_____

Select one of these" experiments in change" to do within the next week.

❏ *Being Straightforward*

Keep a record of situations at work in which you were not up-front with someone else—when you hinted and hedged, but didn't say what was on your mind or when you brought up a different subject than the one you really wanted to raise. Think about the reasons why you were evasive. Select one or two situations that might arise again and plan how you can be more straightforward. Then try out your plan and see how it goes.

❏ *Refusing Unwanted Requests*

Make a list of requests people make of you that are a burden. Review the list and select one or two requests that you will refuse in the next week. Think about how you will politely, but firmly, inform someone of your need to say "no," then carry out your plan. What happened? Did you feel less guilty than you thought you would?

❏ *Making Clear Requests*

Review the requests you want to make of others to help you meet your own needs at work. Select one or two. Get clear in your mind what you specifically want. Formulate each request so that it is as reasonable as possible for the person you will ask; then make your request(s). Did you get a positive response? Are you happy with the support you obtained?

❏ *Responding to Objections*

Take one of the following strategies and practice it for one week with a variety of people in various work situations. Work on it until it becomes second-nature:

- Repeat yourself rather than respond to someone's remarks.

- Avoid arguments with others by using phrases such as "That may be," "We see it differently," and "That's true, and. . . ."

- Give brief, nonapologetic explanations for your position.

Think about some words of advice you would give yourself as you apply this training session.

Imagine that you are creating a bumper sticker on the back of your car that contains this message. (Well-known ones are "Think Globally, Act Locally" or "Question Authority.") Don't try to capture the entire essence of this session. Focus on one key learning.

Enter your message below.

SPEAKING UP WITHOUT PUTTING OTHERS DOWN

Many organizations are not places where you can speak freely. There are several reasons why this is so. Among them, consider the following:

- When you speak frankly to a person in your personal life, there's a good chance what you say goes no further than the two of you. In organizations, what one person says is often passed along to others. Unless you've requested that something you say be held in confidence, sooner or later, it is mentioned to a third party and the whole office knows. Knowing that, most people censor what they say.

- For an organization's culture to work, there must be an adequate amount of agreement and conformity. The positive term for this is "organizational alignment." Sometimes, however, things go too far. People are afraid to disagree with or object to the party line.

- Today's organizations depend on teamwork and collaboration. Unfortunately, when individuals speak up, they are sometimes accused of not being "team players" when, in fact, they are simply not acting like "people pleasers."

What happens when you and others in your organization don't speak up? You suffer in silence and others are not privy to your feelings and needs. You seethe inside and feel less positive about your job. Others are denied your input. You lose and they lose.

Of course, no one needs to express everything that's on his or her mind. The key consideration is how important the matter is to your ability to serve the organization effectively. You are not very helpful to the common cause if, among other things, you. . . .

- Fail to convey your misgivings about how a project is going

- Agree to goals and objectives you really don't support

- Allow others to make requests on your time and energy that impede your job performance

- Brood over your lack of importance to others

- Excuse behavior that should not be tolerated

How, then, do you go about the sensitive task of "speaking up" so that you and others benefit? The first challenge is to communicate honestly without being hurtful or putting others on the defensive. Following are some suggestions.

Stand Behind What You Say

Make "I" statements when you want to share your feelings or views. If what you mean is *"I don't think we are getting at the core problem of why sales are down,"* don't say: *"Don't you think there are other factors at work here?"* If you are not sure you have been understood, don't say, *"Do you understand?"* Say instead, *"Am I making sense?"*

Everyone is entitled to a perspective. You don't have to air all of your views all of the time, but when you choose to share what's on your mind, accept the fact that it is *your* opinion, not the absolute truth. Say, *"I think this plan is misguided,"* rather than *"This plan is misguided."* Or *"It seems to me that you are trying to control things too tightly,"* rather than *"You're micro-managing!"*

At the same time, avoid qualifying what you think and feel by using phrases like *kind of, sort of, maybe, really,* or *a little* as you make your point. Don't hedge so much. Be loud and clear:

- *"I'm angry."*

- *"I disagree."*

- *"I don't believe you."*

- *"I admire you."*

- *"I think you're correct."*

Make the Listener Comfortable

Talking straight doesn't mean you have to make others defensive. People get uptight when their control is removed or when their self-esteem is under attack. Avoid words like *always* and *never* . . . even when you are complimenting someone. It's a no-brainer to realize how infuriating it is to say to someone: *"You never say anything nice."* But think about the impact of saying to someone, *"You always do a great job!"* You might be implying that the person had better not have a "bad day."

Another coaching tip is to describe someone's behavior without interpreting it. Better to say: *"You are not letting me finish"* than *"You don't care what I have to say, do you?"* Don't control the solution by saying something like: *"We must stay within our budget,"* when you could share the problem by saying: *"I'm worried that we are over budget. What can we do about it?"*

Let's apply this advice to an everyday situation at work. Imagine that you have been upset about an overly friendly co-worker (a "schmoozer") who hangs around you a lot, tells you about matters that are not work-related, and doesn't give you enough privacy or time to do your work. Sometimes you get rid of the "schmoozer" with some excuse, but he doesn't pick up on your hints. You realize that the time has come to address the problem. How might you deal with this situation?

You might continue hinting with words like: *"Boy, is it 11 o'clock already?"* Or you might gamely try to continue working in his presence, giving him just the slightest attention until he picks up the hint. Or, in frustration, you might try a little veiled ridicule or sarcasm like *"Don't you ever have work to do?"* Instead, consider a more straightforward approach. Concentrate on what you are experiencing because of his schmoozing, such as *"I have a problem. When you come to visit me, I enjoy our conversations, but I get behind in my work. It would help me if we could 'shoot the breeze' over lunch."*

Assertiveness Begins Within

It's hard enough to speak freely about your ideas and feelings. It's even tougher when you are asserting your needs. For example, others may want something from you and you would rather not do it (your boss wants you to undertake an assignment that is not a good use of your talents) or you want something from others that may be an imposition (assistance in completing a project).

Unless you believe in your right to assert your needs and the value to others if you do, you won't be effective when you try to do it. It's "people smart" to develop your assertiveness skills for many reasons. Here are some benefits that assertive people receive:

- *People respect individuals who are forthright.* When they are straightforward, other people usually admire their courage and personal strength.

- *People adhere to their boundaries and limits.* The quiet firmness of assertive people goes a long way toward influencing others to respect their expectations. Because their style does not arouse anger, others are more willing to comply.

- *They often get what they want without destroying the relationship.* Assertive people stand up for themselves but in a manner that does not demean the other person. As a result, the other person accepts the assertive person's limits as a necessary component of the relationship. When treated poorly, others will shy away from the relationship.

- *They have a strong sense of personal power.* When people smart individuals assert what they need and obtain a positive response, they become more confident. This enables them to act assured the next time. Their self-assurance builds on itself.

- *They are rarely abused by aggressive people.* Assertive people don't fall prey to bullies because they are adept at setting limits and protecting themselves. They are clear about their own rights, as well as those of others, and stand their ground with grace and tact.

- *They have a grip on their emotions under stress.* No one is immune to becoming emotional under trying circumstances, but assertive people know how to re-adjust and relax because they keep focused on their goals and stay on track.

- *Their calmness helps others to be calm.* When you yell at someone, he or she might be inclined to yell back. When you are calm, the other person is inclined to be calm. Even when someone is yelling at you, if your response is calm, the person starts to bring it down a notch or two. The ability of assertive people to remain calm under fire keeps everyone calm.

Guidelines for Asserting Your Needs

Before saying a word, you need to be *clear* up-front about exactly what you want to accomplish. Let's apply this to the following example:

> *You are feeling overwhelmed because your boss gives more assignments than you can handle effectively. Before you speak up, consider first what you want to request: Fewer assignments? His priority list? Additional resources? Advance warning? Ideally, you want all of these things, but what's your realistic goal? That's what getting clear is all about.*

People also need to know *how insistent you are.* If you think of your possible level of insistence as being on a 1 to 10 scale, how strongly do you feel about your present need? If you feel that your need is a 10, but you only sound like a 1, the other person doesn't know how important the issue is to you. On the other hand, if you sound like a 10 all the time, you become like the boy who cried wolf, and you lose credibility. Consider the following example:

> *You are continually asked to provide computer assistance to others in your department who are not as adept as you. If you are basically okay with providing this assistance, you might respond to the next request by saying:* "Okay. I'll help you out, but would appreciate it if I could teach you how to do it yourself sometimes. How does that sound?" *If you are feeling a bit put off by the requests of others, you might say:* "I need to let you know that I'm feeling overwhelmed by the requests I've been getting. I'll give you some help when I can, but I will have to say no sometimes and I hope you'll understand." *If you feel that the entire situation is out of hand, you might insist:* "Sorry, folks. I must say no to your requests for computer assistance. It's all I can do to complete what's on my plate. Please ask for help elsewhere."

Having become clear about where you stand and how insistent you are, you are in a much better position to express yourself calmly and confidently. Here are some tips to help you speak up clearly . . . and with tact.

Take a Deep Breath and Slow Yourself Down.   If you rush yourself, you're likely to come across with little confidence. Your body language is key. People pick up subtle cues in your body language that suggest that they can get the upper hand. Tone of voice, gestures, and eye contact greatly affect the way another person decides how insistent you are . . . no matter how carefully you select your words.

Use Clear, Direct Statements.   Having clarified what you want, you are now ready to express your need to the other person. Don't beat around the bush. That makes others suspicious and defensive. Go through the front door instead of the back! Use phrases like:

- *"I would appreciate it if you would. . . [call me first thing in the morning]."*

- *"I will not. . . [be able to come to the meeting]."*

- *"It would be great if you . . . [could give me a day's notice]."*

- *"I will have to. . . [turn down your request]."*

- *"Please. . . [tell me when you are ready for the next assignment]."*

- *"I would prefer that you. . . [get assistance from someone with more free time]."*

- *"It works best for me if. . . [you put it in writing]."*

- *"I've decided not to. . . [volunteer this time]."*

Avoid such questions as *"Don't you think you could have informed me first?"* Rhetorical appeals almost never get results. To help you avoid them (if the habit is well-engrained), *focus on what you want* from the other person whenever he or she is doing something that interferes with your needs. Often, there is a tendency to *comment on the person's behavior* instead.

Explain Your Reasons . . . Briefly.   Usually, asserting your needs requires an explanation. The key is to explain yourself so that you are informative, without being defensive. Give a brief, respectful, honest explanation for your position, as in, *"I don't want to work this weekend because I haven't had quality time with my family recently."* Too often, however, people go on and on, justifying themselves as if their position is not valid until others agree with them (which they seldom do). If you stop, rather than go on and on, you give breathing room for the other person to reply and even to object. Don't be concerned about that. You can't filibuster forever. Giving room for a response shows your confidence that you can handle whatever happens.

Don't Become Defensive or Caught Up in Power Struggles, or Blow Your Cool.   If you find that the other person is not initially responsive to your needs, avoid arguing. Calmly restate what you want, trying to say the same thing in new words.

For example, imagine that you asked a colleague to send you a report you need immediately and you didn't receive it. You might say something like: *"I thought you agreed to send me that report. It was important to me. Please keep your word. I count on it."* If you get objections, use phrases like:

- *"That may be."*

- *"We see it differently."*

- *"That's true, and. . . ."*

- *"I realize how important this is to you, and. . . ."*

Here is an illustration of how these tips can be followed.

Timothy is getting ready to leave for the evening. Alyssa, his project leader, approaches him about working on the project over the weekend.

Alyssa: *"Timothy, I need you to come in to work again this weekend. We have that deadline looming!"*

Timothy: *"I thought last weekend was the last time. We have worked every weekend for a month. My family will not be happy."*

Alyssa: *"Timothy, when you signed onto this project, you said you could work some weekends."*

Timothy: *"Alyssa, you're right. I said some weekends, not every weekend. Please ask for more time on this project or find additional time during the day. I am not willing to work another weekend."*

Alyssa (backing off when confronted with Timothy's assertiveness): *"Okay. I hear you. I'm glad you spoke up. We'll just have to ask for more time on the project."*

Three Challenging Situations

Below are three situations that may have occurred in your own work. Read the question posed in each situation and see what an effective solution looks like.

Situation 1

"A combination of business travel and working overtime is causing me to spend so much time away from my family that my kids barely recognize me and my wife hardly speaks to me. How can I get my boss to be more reasonable in her expectations of me?"

When your job consistently stretches into extra hours and miles, the first thing to do is to *assess the situation.* Consider whether there are compelling business rationales for the demands your boss is placing on you, whether others are sharing the load in an equitable way, and whether it was clear up-front that your job would require this much travel and overtime. Based on your assessment, decide on the position you will take with your boss. Do you want to just plant a seed and give him or her time to re-think expectations of you? Or are you prepared to insist on a change, even if it means you begin looking for another job?

Based on your assessment, your next step is to *speak up* and state your position calmly and clearly to your boss. Maybe this entails saying no to a specific request (*"I'm sorry, Alice, but I just can't work this weekend. It's my daughter's high school graduation and we've made plans. I'll be glad to put in some extra time during the week on this project"*). Or perhaps you would prefer to negotiate the general issue of your boss's demands (*"Alice, I'd like to discuss the amount of overtime and travel I'm putting in. Perhaps you're not aware of how many hours it's been coming to recently. I'm seriously concerned that I'm on overload and it's affecting the quality of my work"*). In sharing a rationale for your boss to reconsider his or her demands, you are more likely to be persuasive if your reasons are business-related, rather than personal. Perhaps you can show your boss that the travel and overtime have negative consequences for other projects or business relationships.

When you negotiate with your boss, try to *suggest alternatives* that will meet his or her needs. Is it possible to recruit a colleague to share some of the load? Some people like business travel more than others. Are there other projects—even very unpopular ones—that you might volunteer for in lieu of travel or overtime? Could you do some overtime work at home, so that you at least have a little more time with your family?

While there is no guarantee that your boss will respond favorably to your appeal, it's worth trying. You'll be clearer about where you stand, and your family will appreciate your efforts.

Situation 2

"It seems like I'm always the one who puts in the extra time and effort when my team has a deadline. Why don't the others ever offer to pitch in and do their fair share?"

Your co-workers might be willing to pull their weight, but they cannot read your mind. Although the inequities in the situation are obvious to you, they might not be obvious to them. Maybe your colleagues simply don't notice your efforts or, if they do, perhaps they tell themselves you prefer to do the work yourself.

If you haven't been up-front and clear with your co-workers, it's time to tell them how you feel and what you want from them. First think through your position: exactly what are you seeking from each of your colleagues? Decide how insistent you're prepared to be, and be ready to give a brief rationale for your request. Once you're clear on your position, speak up. Stay calm and confident and don't blow your cool if you encounter resistance. Instead, stand your ground, acknowledge objections, and reiterate what you want: *"Doris, I understand that this is a bad week for you. But Frank expects our report on Friday and it's going to take some overtime by both of us to get it done. Which section will you take?"*

Another approach is to sit down with your co-workers and give them some feedback about the way you see your respective contributions; for example, *"Doris, it seems to me that I'm usually the one who volunteers to work late when there's a deadline. I'm willing to do my share, but do you think we could talk about some ways to share the load more equitably?"* Don't wait for a crisis in order to do this. Pick a quiet time and calmly share your perspective of the situation and how it affects you and the team's productivity. Offer specific examples and suggestions for improvement. Then check out how your co-workers are responding and ask what they would be willing to do to change things.

Situation 3

"I hate to admit this, but once in a while I just lose it with some of my staff. Last week I yelled at my assistant and called her incompetent after she mixed up some appointments in my schedule. I know I need to find a better way to handle my anger when their behavior gets to me. But how?"

People sometimes think that only the meek need to develop assertiveness skills. But the reality is that aggression misses the mark just as much as passivity does. And because hostility is more conspicuous than wimping out, it can get you into hot water more quickly. Even when you're the boss, you can't get away with losing your cool.

Ironically, many people who tend to blow their tops need to become more adept at expressing their wants, needs, and limits with others. By speaking up calmly and clearly, you can take the guesswork out of communicating your expectations to others, rather than hoping for the best and accumulating resentments. Think through the "fine print" before you give assignments to your direct reports. Spell out the specific "who, what, when, where, and how" details of what you want done, in advance. Invite their questions so that you can clarify any misunderstandings up-front.

In addition to managing your staff more effectively, you can do a better job at managing your emotional responses. Learn to recognize your personal warning signs of anger building, whether it's clenching your jaw muscles, knots in your stomach, or feeling like you want to throw something. Become aware of the "tapes" you typically play in your head that keep your anger fueled (such as thoughts like *"She always does this"* or *"Mistakes like this will sink the whole project"*). When you feel yourself building up steam, change your tape. See if you can think more neutrally about the situation, instead of taking things too personally or catastrophizing. Take a few deep breaths, a drink of water, or a walk around the block and *don't* try to talk with the person who's angered you until you are calm. Try writing a script of what you can say and editing out anything inflammatory before you approach the person to speak. Practice expressing disappointment or dissatisfaction by making "I" rather than "you" statements. *"I'm unhappy with this report"* sounds better than *"You did this wrong."*

Notes

Notes

Notes

Notes

Notes